Productivity:
The 8 Laws of Productivity
Learn How to Be Productive and Get More Done to Increase Success

By: Gerald Campbell

Copyright 2016 by Gerald Campbell All Rights Reserved

This document is geared toward providing helpful and supportive information about the topic covered in the following chapters. This work is sold with the idea that the author is not required to provide any type of qualified service. If a person seeks to obtain personal counseling where the law requires a professional, such as a lawyer or a doctor for example, then that person should do so.

No part of this book may be reproduced in any manner whatsoever without written permission. Unauthorized reproduction of this work is illegal. No part of this book may be scanned, uploaded, or posted on the internet without the author's permission.

The information provided in this document is stated to be truthful. Any liability by use or abuse of direction, suggestions, or guidance is the responsibility of the reader. Under no circumstances is any legal responsibility held against the publisher or author for any damages or loss due to the information in these pages. The information found herein is for information purpose only and does not offer a guarantee of result or outcome for any purpose

Table of Contents

Introduction

Law 1: Jump From Your Starting Point

Law 2: Make it Manageable

Law 3: Start Small and Make Your Goal Reachable

Law 4: Master, Mold, and Prototype

Law 5: The Habit Building Process

Law 6: Cut The Excess

Law 7: Rule Maker Not Rule Breaker

Law 8: Never Give Up & Do It Again

Conclusion

Other Books in the 8 Laws to Self-Improvement Series

Introduction

Welcome to the secrets of the successful mindset that will lead you toward the habits of greater productivity. What is it that hinders people from getting over that motivational hump that keeps them from the level of productivity that one desires? How does a person continue to keep up a productive work pace if they've already started off on the right step? Hopefully, we can help you answer some of these questions.

If you are a follower of the 8 Laws Series, then you will be looking forward to the **Focus Treasure** for this volume. A Focus Treasure is an American patriot from whom we will draw insight with their words and life experiences, and we will think about how that person relates to the lesson pertaining to the topic of the book. For the 8 Laws of Productivity, there is only one man who stands separate from every other busy inventor who ever lived in the heart of America, Thomas Edison. In recent years, Thomas Edison has been the topic of controversy pertaining to the origins of his inventions and the methods he used to obtain patents. Regardless of this debate, he was undeniably a forward thinking power house who possessed the characteristics of a leader, and who got more done for the twenty-first century than any other inventor of his time. Thomas Edison treasured his creative intellect, and rarely stopped mulling over ideas. He identified with the hardworking man who wasn't afraid to get down in the dirt and fix machines and get his knees muddy, and he held work ethic to a high standard. He was mentally on the go, pressing forward, and always creating. He left behind solid ideas about the values of productivity and work, as well as inspiring words to keep the next generation inventing and exploring. It is for these reasons that Thomas Edison has become our Focus Treasure for the 8 Laws of Productivity.

Focus Treasure: Thomas Edison

Thomas Edison was born in Milan, Ohio in 1847. An American businessman and inventor,

he was responsible for the mass production of inventions that raised the quality of life for millions of people around the world, not the least of his success was the incandescent light bulb. Although he invented a few well known things, he was also responsible for over two thousand inventions in his life time and held patents for over half of them. He progressed in his years with acclaim, rubbing elbows with the important business men of his time like Henry Ford and Harvey Firestone. He was well liked by his peers before he passed from this world in 1931, but not before being given several recognitions for his work, including a Congressional Gold Medal.

One of the outstanding characteristics of Thomas Edison was his work ethic and his attitude on always moving forward with his busy production line. He was also known for his dedicated commitment to his customers. He left us with terrific insight on the mind of an inventing genius, and he left us with ideas on how we can apply that insight, motivation, and work ethic to our everyday tasks.

8 Laws of Productivity

Law 1

The 1st Law: Jump from Your Starting Point

"Being busy does not always mean real work. The object of all work is production or accomplishment and to either of these ends there must be forethought, system, planning, intelligence, and honest purpose, as well as perspiration. Seeming to do is not doing."
- Thomas Edison

Hesitate? Procrastinate? No! Don't Wait!

One can sit down with successful entrepreneurs and ask the same thing over and over again. What is it that separates you and your success from the guy who tried to do the same things you do and never made it to your level? Almost always, the business man will tell you the same thing. Well, he will say thoughtfully, I just actually did the thing I set out to do. I just did it.

It doesn't matter if you interview two or hundreds of creative professional men and women, you will hear the same theme attributed to their success. They took a bias toward action.

When starting off in the dreaming and planning stages of a new business or venture, these people moved through the 'day dreaming' process quickly. Their minds morphed into the planning process and then into the action phase. While other people, who were less successful, splashed around in the kiddy pool of their dreams and ideas, and lounged in their thoughts, they never took action deeper into their plans. This leaves a vacant space in their accomplishments, while others will see it as an opportunity to move in.

If you want to be one of the movers and the shakers of the world, you must challenge yourself to take action sooner rather than later. The minute that you start acting (e.g. building that actual mock up, sharing that physical prototype with your co-inventors, yes, even if your co-inventor is your mother), you start getting support in the form of valuable feedback that will help progress your original idea – and carry forward with a more informed perspective.

Planning and preparing is the first step to manifesting your ideas into reality. When getting off to a start on any new venture or work idea, it helps to do a little self-internalizing at first. What kind of worker are you? You can benefit from exploring this idea so that you can start off by putting yourself in the right kind of environment early on.

Recognize what kind of worker you are:

The Planner: The Planner is an important part of a team. He or she needs the support of his team mates to follow through with their responsibilities so s/he can focus on the details of a project. This person thrives on organization, sequence, and the minutia of a project. They enjoy detailed thinking. They often need space and quiet and introspect. The Planner will immerse themselves in a project and focus on every little detail. These will be the important details and the small touches that brings craftsmanship and artistry to a completed job.

Planners love excel spread sheets, calendars, and organized 'to-do' lists. They thrive on these things and make it a part of their identity.

Planners are predictable to the point of being accused of boring. They do not like surprise or spontaneity. They even miss opportunities, sometimes, because they don't like to deviate from their well thought out plans. These are the people who write a to-do list of things that need to be done, and then a to-do list of things that have already been completed just so they can see that things are crossed off the list. They look forward to the schedules that they create, their well-prepared plans are the foundation of their confidence. They are timely with their follow ups. They want you to get to the point; they'll read the fine print later. They hate attending a meeting without an agenda. Their emails are micro detailed, often including bullet points and clearly directed point by point steps.

Planners bring the following skills to the table:

- Action orientation and practicality
- Finding flaws in the details that have been over looked by other team members
- Organizing and maintaining data and project plans

Planners will love the following tools:

These are additional online tools that are available for team workers to get through their daily tasks.

Some are software that can be purchased, while some are free downloads

- Agendas: Creates interactive agendas and broadcasts them to iPad users.
- Toodledo: Lets you make custom lists, create structured outlines, views tasks on a calendar.
- HabitForge: A habit-forming tool designed around accountability that includes daily check-ins and progress reports.
- Objectiveli: Manages and track goals in real time.
- Low-tech tools like label makers, file folders, filing cabinets, drawer organizers, pen holders, and other office organizational supplies.

The Prioritizer: The Prioritizer is the one who loves the logical, the analytical, and the fact based material. They require evidence and do not take leaps on an assumption. They prefer realistic and predictable thinking. It is important for the Prioritizer to be efficient. They self-assign deadlines and pay attention to their work so that they can predict how long it will take them to complete their own tasks. This way they can schedule and arrange with predictability and confidence. This person is goal oriented and have the personality to apply laser-like focus when they have set their sights on a task. They have never met a goal they did not like.

These individuals are so focused on the execution of their project that they don't spend much time or energy on *how* it is completed. At times they have a tendency to be pragmatic and rigid, and may be known in the office setting for their myopic drive and competitiveness. They hate idle chit-chat, extra fluff, missing data, or oversharing of anything personal or irrelevant to the task at hand. Their written communications are often only a few sentences, or when possible, as minimal as a few letters.

Prioritizers bring the following to the table:

- Analyzing data
- Critical analysis and logical problem solving
- Goal orientation, consistency, and decisiveness

Tools the Prioritizer will love:

These are additional online tools that are available for team workers to get through their daily tasks. Some are software that can be purchased, while some have free downloads

- 42Goals: Tracks your daily goals and keeps a log of your daily activities.

- Daytum: Helps you collect, categorize, and communicate any and all of your data.

- Moosti: A timer-tool based on the Pomodoro Technique.
- Witty Parrott: Enables you to create snippets of content once and then seamlessly reuse or share them.
- Wunderlist: Tracks and reminds you of your to-dos.
- Classic low-tech tools, like legal pads and a label maker.

The Arranger: An Arranger prefers supportive, expressive, and emotional thinking. They are the ultimate team player and excel at partnering with colleagues to get work done. They are a natural communicator and deftly facilitate project meetings. They hate when people lack that personal touch or rely too heavily on data or facts. Arrangers are talkers; they love stories, eye-to-eye contact, expressing concern for others, and asking questions about the way a project or task helps others. They have been known to need to institute a personal chat budget, only allowing a few minutes of chit chat during work hours, and have to avoid adding one more person to the cc: line on their email messages.

Arrangers bring to the table:

- Anticipating how others will feel and understanding their underlying emotions
- Facilitating team interaction
- Persuading and selling ideas

Tools the Arranger will love:

- focus@will: A neuroscience-based music service that helps you focus and retain information when working, studying, writing and reading.
- stickK: A habit forming tool that focuses on incentives, accountability and community (and if you are unsuccessful, stickK lets your friends know).

- workshifting: A resource site that shares ideas to help you shift when, where and how you work.
- Redbooth: A complete collaboration and communication solution that enables you to leverage your existing work flow infrastructure like Outlook, MSProject, Box, Gmail, DropBox, Evernote, and more.
- Visually and kinesthetically pleasing office supplies, things like Moleskin notebooks with unlined pages, and pens in a variety of ink colors.

The Visualizer: A Visualizer prefers holistic, intuitive, integrating, and synthesizing thinking. They thrive under pressure and are easily bored if they are not juggling multiple, diverse projects. A Visualizer focuses on the big-picture and broad concepts making connections. At times, they have a tendency to overlook details and tend to value the possibilities over process. Their excessive spontaneity and impulsiveness can lead to breakthrough ideas, but can also derail project plans at times. A Visualizer has probably not seen the surface of their desk in years because if something is out of sight, it is out of mind. And, their emails tend to be long, filled with concepts and ideas.

Visualizers bring the following to the table:

- Innovation; serving as a catalyst for change
- Creative problem solving
- Ability to envision the future, recognize new opportunities and integrate ideas and concepts

Tools the Visualizer Will Love:

- Lifetick: A highly visual dreams achievement tool where you can create and add to your lifelong "bucket list."
- iThoughts HD: A digital mind-mapping tool.

- AdBlock Plus: A tool that blocks ads automatically and speeds up page download times.
- ZenPen: A tool that creates a minimalist writing zone where you can block out all distractions.
- Visually vibrant, low-tech tools: multicolored Post-It notes, colored folders, notebooks with unlined pages, pens in a variety of ink colors, large white boards, baskets, folders, and bags and clipboards for keeping papers visible while still organized.

Law 2
The 2nd Law: Make It Manageable

"Nearly every man who develops an idea works it up to the point where it looks impossible, and then he gets discouraged. That's not the place to become discouraged."
- Thomas Edison

Break big, long-term projects into smaller chunks or "phases."

Now that you have decided to take action on that big dream, you want to prevent the chance that you will become overwhelmed when you realize your idea is a little more ambitious than you realized. If you aren't careful, you can find yourself paralyzed, not knowing where to begin, if your project seems too big.

Taking on too large of a project runs the risk of a few hazards that can burn your dreams down before you begin. First, if your project has too many ideas that off shoot from the main concept, you will quickly become disorganized and won't know where to begin. Second, if the result and reward of building that dream is too far away you can easily lose motivation, and without the desire to continue your project is sure to fail. Finally, if you start with an idea that is too big, your mind is less likely to conceptualize it as a tangible desire that you can actually obtain.

The solution to this problem is an easy concept, but this is where the planning and decision making begins. To help manage expectations and stay motivated for long term or even multi-year endeavors, break each project into smaller chunks that only take a few weeks or a month to complete. The dual benefit of this approach is that it makes the project feel more manageable, and you will need to provide incremental rewards throughout the project. It's crucial to pause periodically to take an audit of what has been accomplished – even if there's still a long way to go.

What does it mean to make a large project manageable? By manageable we mean arranging these already small tasks into a flow line of organization. This step takes a little more advanced thinking, and this is usually where your team developer, or project manager, will be hired to step in.

Now, depending on the nature of your work, you may not have a team manager, you may be the boss of your own self. If that's the case, the key concept here is responsibility and being able to see the whole picture. Once you have your work broken down into doable projects, and you have committed yourself to focus at a set time to complete the little tasks, and you are willing to do this on schedule repetitively, you need to realistically organize these tasks so they fit together and flow in a way that makes sense.

Breaking the time spent on your project into chunks can help with getting the job done faster.

Blocking out your time into work bursts is another way of getting through a big project in small chunks. It might seem to others that you are doing too many things at once, or are easily distracted, but one way to break up projects that are difficult to complete is not to see the project in terms of begging and end. Try to see your project in the form of a 20-minute work burst. Sit down with the intent to commit your full attention and energy for 20 minutes and follow through as thoroughly as possible until the 20 minutes is complete. Don't worry how close you are to completion, only worry that you say focused and consistent for your committed block of time. Once your time is up, remove yourself from the project and go do something else. This will prevent fatigue and boredom. Most importantly, it will prevent those times when you force yourself to sit in front of a task only to zone out and get nothing done while you stare at how much work you have in front of you. Time chunking is an effective way to break a large project into smaller chunks.

Both of these methods require that you stay aware of your deadlines and work within the boundaries of your requirements that are needed to complete the entire task. This requires that you can see both the small details and the large picture of the project as a whole. Now, what do you do about breaking your objective down into a manageable size if you are not in the beginning stages. What if your project is already massive, and you are hired in as a project manager, or you are a new business consultant hired to look over a business and make it more efficient? The 3rd Law will provide the next solution for you.

Law 3
The 3rd Law: Start Small and Make Your Goal Reachable

"To invent, you need a good imagination and a pile of junk."

- Thomas Edison

So, now we know, that starting out small is a useful strategy, so you don't lose your steam before you start. When our ideas are still in our head, we tend to think big dream fantasies. We imagine some accomplishment or goal as it would be a finished project. We imagine that fully built dream home or bustling business. The downside is that this thinking might make a barrier to entry that keeps us just a little out of reach from starting that dream. To avoid "big dream paralysis," pare your idea down to a small, immediately actionable concept. Big goals and big projects often require big first steps, but being overwhelmed by the idea of all that work is normal. You may not have enough time in the day to get everything you want done, or maybe you have a lot of prep-work to get off to a solid start. Don't get stuck sitting in fear unable to get started because you're afraid that you don't know where to start, start small and take small bites out of a big project in incremental steps. The principle of working in small with easily-completed steps isn't anything new, but when applied to your 'to-do' list it can be a productive tool. You now fully understand how this strategy is used when beginning a fresh project, now let's discuss how we tweak this same strategy when we approach a project or task that has already been fully built and developed and needs an over haul for improvement.

The productivity and business developments of American manufacturing began to stretch its tentacles and leave influences in the far corners of the world. Thomas Edison began to reach overseas with his patents and explore the idea of bringing his businesses to other markets. Likewise, he drew many curious people from other countries to work with him. A young Japanese man named Kunihiko Iwadare worked in Thomas Edison's factories at General Electric. Prior to going back to his country, he learned technical skills on manufacturing and assembly line work that he incorporated into a company that he founded, today called Nippon Electric.

The Japanese used their own cultural influences on development and business, and combined it with the ingenuity of the new century that they learned during the American manufacturing explosion to develop methods for productivity. These had proven to be efficient and successful techniques not only in commercial business but also in individual small business. The method called Kaizen has been widely adapted from the East into the American work strategy today.

Kaizen

Kaizen is a Japanese philosophy, and the word is Japanese for "improvement," so this means you make all small micro changes to get things moving, but the overall goal is to make the whole project better. It's based on making little changes on an ongoing basis: always improving productivity and effectiveness while reducing waste. It's a soft, gradual method and the concept can be applied to any aspect of your life.

Additionally, Kaizen is about creating whole systems and processes, and continuously tweaking these processes to get the best results and to reduce lost time. One example is to create a morning routine and modify it slightly every few days to create improved results. By the end of a few weeks you have created an entirely new routine that looked nothing like the one you started with, only you did it gradually and it didn't disrupt your whole life.

Examples:

Do you spend less time in the bathroom getting ready if you keep your face wash, tooth brush, and toothpaste on the bathroom counter instead of storing these somewhere else in the room?

What if you also put an umbrella stand next to your coat rack by the door?

What if you hang a key cupboard by the door and make sure to always leave your keys there when you enter the house so you can easily find them in the morning when you're leaving for work?

What if you put coffee and water in the coffee maker the night before and set the timer instead of doing it in the morning?

You can see that these are very small trivial actions. Just about anything you can think of during the course of your daily routine can be improved continuously, if you try to make these small changes in little steps.

Make things easy for yourself:

Set yourself up to succeed by breaking your changes down into small, blocks at a time. Don't try to tweak to many little things at once. If there's a project you're resisting, or if you're just having a lazy day, allow yourself to make changes at a pace that feels comfortable. Create momentum by checking off small items from your list. Congratulate yourself for each item you complete, however small they may be.

Also, use the concept of Kaizen is to make small, constant changes to your life so that you're always on the road of continuous improvement. It's not just change for the sake of it. Since, you are doing these little moves in small steps, if you try one that you discover doesn't do much for your goal, you can always roll back that change and go in a different direction. This way you have disrupted little in the overall scheme of things.

When you are working through your to-do list, do small things incrementally as progress towards your goal. If you do it this way, you'll notice things so small that it feels easy, and you aren't caught up in paralysis or excuses for why you're not working.

When the task is so small that it seems almost meaningless, the subconscious mind offers almost no resistance to it, since it doesn't consider it an arduous chore, and you find it easy to do.

After a few days of achieving little successes, the subconscious mind starts enjoying the task so much, it automatically starts wanting more. While before, even one minute of an undesirable task may have seemed like enough, you now find yourself doing these tasks for longer periods of time – first five minutes, then ten minutes and then eventually hours.

Many people have a list of ambitious projects they plan to complete, such as the following:

- Write a bestselling novel
- Run a marathon
- Start an online diary blog and build subscribers
- Invest a large amount of money and live off the interest
- Donate a full weekend to charity

It is good to be a believer in aiming high. Too many people find that they underestimate their abilities. However, sometimes they also overestimate what they can do in the short run. You can set ambitious goals for yourself over the long haul, but in the short run, you need to keep things small and within realistic perspective.

Let's look deeper at three ways to achieve your goals by thinking small. These three ways are the following:

- Break big projects down into small doable action steps
- Make micro movements
- Reward yourself for small achievements

Prepare Big Projects into Small Action Steps

As we've stated, when you're feeling overwhelmed by a large project or goal that you need to tackle, make your action steps smaller and easier. How do you know where to start breaking these projects down? One clue that will let you know that you need to break your goal down into smaller chunks is that you find yourself procrastinating. Procrastination is often caused by the feeling of being overwhelmed.

By breaking big projects down into small action steps, you can realistically accomplish things that others only talk about. Here are some examples:

Write That Book Your Dreamed About

Louis L'Amoure was an American novelist who specialized in historical fiction set in the Southwestern United States. He was a prolific author and over the course of his career he wrote more than 100 novels and short western stories.

In fact, L'Amoure wrote more than three full-length novels a year for 30 years. Once a reporter asked him: "How do you get the inspiration for so many villains and heroes?" And he answered: "Victory is not won in miles, but in inches".

Going from Couch Potato to Running a 5K

Another example of the importance of breaking projects down into small steps is "The

Couch to 5K Running Plan". It offers a running schedule to help the non-athletic types take up running. The plan has helped thousands to go from running zero miles to running three miles, in just two months.

We all know that a lot of people are turned off from running by trying to start too fast. They go out and jog for as long as they can endure on the very first day, and wake up the next day with every ache and pain imaginable. Then they wonder why on earth anyone would want to take up running.

An example of this running method looks like this:

- It starts off the first day alternating just 60 seconds of jogging with 90 seconds of walking for a total of 20 minutes.
- Then, gradually, throughout the next nine weeks the jogging time is increased and the walking time is decreased.

- By the end of the two months you're jogging for 30 minutes straight, which is basically the equivalent of three miles or 5 kilometers.

A person can go from couch potato to running a 5K in just two months by breaking down the task into small, doable steps.

Marketing Your Business

A third example is marketing your business. Suppose that you want more clients for your business, but you're not doing anything about it. Why? Anyone who's ever tried this knows that, "finding new clients" is a pretty large a task, and you're not sure how to tackle it.

Ask yourself: "What's the first thing I need to do?" It could be: "Contact leads". If this task still looks too large, you can make it even smaller: "Identify leads".

Another item you can add is "Look for networking events I can attend." You could also add, "Identify former clients and ask for referrals." These are examples of small, specific activities you can schedule and carry out, rather than staring blankly at vague umbrella concept of: "Find new clients".

Micro movements – Make It Small Enough to Get You Going

If you're having one of those days in which you just can't get yourself to move, or there's a project that you just can't seem to get started on, try micro actions. A micro actions consist of itsy-bitsy-teeny-weeny movements. More specifically, a micro action is a small burst of work that consists of working on a project within a span of 5 minutes or less. This is perfect with those with low motivation or a short attention span. This is also a technique that builds up over time and helps breakthrough in those moments of procrastination.

Additionally, it's important to record each micro movement with a day and time. For example, if one wants to create a new craft project, one would write down the following:

1. Call Sarah Wed. 10am ask where she got the great checkered gingham
2. Thu 11am, put fabric near sewing machine
3. Fri 4pm, draw two types of curtain ideas
4. Sat 2pm, assemble design for 5 minutes
5. Sun 5pm sew a new curtain valance.

Although using micro movements means that you'll proceed slowly, it's a much better alternative than never getting started. Just go slow and steady.

Reward Yourself for Small Achievements

Small victories create psychological momentum. The principle of using small wins to build psychological momentum was presented in a Ph.D. dissertation at Stanford University in 1977.

When someone praises you, you feel good because your brain produces a chemical called dopamine. When you praise yourself by checking off a completed action step, you get the same physiological result. As you achieve one small win after another, you find it easier and easier to take the action steps that generate the wins.

If you can get yourself to start ticking off small items, it will get you rolling and will continue ticking off items. In addition, giving yourself positive reinforcement after each small achievement will help you even more in keeping the momentum going.

The process to follow is this: break each task down into small action steps; make it easy to identify when you've completed each step; reward yourself for each achievement, even if it's just by acknowledging and congratulating yourself each time you complete an item; and then repeat.

Law 4

The 4th Law: Master, Mold, and Prototype

"I have not failed. I've just found 10,000 ways that won't work."

- Thomas Edison

Trial and error is an essential part of any artistic creators' life. Usually when one executes an idea for the first time, it won't work out in real life the way it did in one's imagination. The important thing is to get the hands on knowledge that is gained during the building process to refine the idea, and create a better version with each attempt until you perfect it into the item or goal that you first imagined.

Famous inventors who are known for coming up with one idea after the next understand that after a while their process becomes a science of steps that produce results. One of those steps is the proto type process. Serial idea-makers all attest: prototyping and iteration is key to transforming a so-so idea into a game-changing product. Rather than being discouraged by your so called "failures," listen closely and learn from them. Next, build a new prototype, then do it again. Sooner or later, you'll find success.

To avoid 'blue sky paralysis,' pare your idea down to a small, immediately executable concept. We have discussed this in the Kaisen technique, but this is also holds effectiveness when it comes to making of your first prototypes.

Create simple objectives for projects, and revisit them regularly.

When working on in-depth projects, we generate lots of new ideas along the way. This can lead to a gradual expansion of the project's goals, or what we call "scope creep." This easily over looked habit can make it impossible to ever really complete anything. The best way to avoid it is to write down a simple statement summarizing your objective at the start of each project. (If you have collaborators, make sure there is agreement about the objective.) And then, this is part everyone seems to forget, review y our objective regularly. When scope creep starts to happen, take notice.

One of Edison's biggest keys to success was his attitude toward failure. He saw failure as an opportunity to learn something and grow and was never discouraged by it.

"Negative results are just what I want. They're just as valuable to me as positive results. I can never find the thing that does the job best until I find the ones that don't." – Thomas Edison

The 5th Law: The Habit Building Process

"I never did anything by accident, nor did any of my inventions come by accident; they came by work."

- Thomas Edison

Work on your project a little bit each day.

With projects that require a serious infusion of creative momentum, such as developing a new business plan, writing a novel, or just learning a new skill, it's incredibly important to maintain momentum. Just as when you run every day, the exercise gets easier and easier, the same thing happens with your brain. Stimulate it regularly each day, and those connections start to flow more freely. The important thing isn't how much you do; it's how often you do it.

Develop a routine.

Part of being able to work on your project a little bit each day is carving out the time to do so. Routines can seem boring and uninspiring, but on the contrary they create a foundation for sparking true insight. The famous Japanese author Haruki Murakami writes about how a rigorous routine – rising at 5am and going to bed at 10pm every day – is crucial to the volume of his creative result.

Another way to look at habit building is in the form of rituals. You already know that breaking your tasks down into small manageable chores will put you in the right frame of mind to think about getting started, but taking a small bite out of a big responsibility isn't going to do much if you don't have a plan from there.

Rituals can help in the form of small repetitive tasks that build up over time making the work you put out build up into a greater accomplishment.

For example: You've decided to write your memoirs of the time you assisted a master hot air balloon piolet. You have so many things to talk about and this book will cover twelve years of your entire life. It seems like a massive daunting task to file all that information and organize it in a way that will entertain people in the same way you remember your profound experience. That's fine. You already know that you don't have to write it in one sitting. You can start small, just write the first chapter about the day you applied for an unusual job.

Of course, this might be the thing you need to get you motivated to start that dream project, but if you don't have a plan from here on out, there is no guarantee you'll ever get past that first chapter. Now, you need to take those bursts of small work sessions and organize them into a predictable schedule. You need to be able to sit down multiple times and do this step until your project is complete. Forming a scheduled ritual is one way to help aid your success in this way.

By a ritual, we mean that you need to develop the mindset that your activity is important and will have a set time and place in your life. If this means that you will write in a thirty minute burst every Monday and Thursday from 8 A.M. to 8:30 A.M. then you need to make yourself sit down and only focus on that task. You need to make the effort a priority.

Not only should you sit down and focus on your task at a set time and location, but you should prevent yourself from becoming paralyzed by making sure you spend this allotted time drilling down to a specific task. For example: you can't both write and edited effectively in thirty minutes and be expected to product results. Maybe sometimes you can do this, occasionally we have a day when we are in full super ninja mode. However, in habit building the key is to find success through repetition. Your plan has to be sustainable every time you sit down to start working. Instead of over loading your work plate at a designated time, you need to assign a focused job with the appropriate amount of work in a given block of time.

By acting out this pre-thought out plan, you have essentially crafted a ritual which must now be put into action.

Another helpful way to sticking to your pre-prepared new habits is a to-do list. Edison was a firm believer in to-do lists and was often heard encouraging his employees to make sure they were prepared at the beginning of their work shifts. He would itemize his daily tasks and even schedule his periodic naps into his day on his to do lists. Some of his more entertaining lists included the inventions that he had planned on the back burner while he was working on others in his laboratory. Here is a peek at one he wrote in June of 1888,

Cotton picker, new phonograph, electrical piano, that is just a sample from one of Edison's crazy to do lists that went on for a total of four long pages, and included scribbles of over 80 inventions.

Edison had what he called an "Idea Quota" that required him to invent a minor invention every 10 days and a major invention every 6 months. He is a testament to what human beings are capable of if we don't settle for low expectations.

"If we did all the things we are capable of, we would literally astound ourselves." – Thomas Edison

It is also possible that his high expectations and specific deadlines were the pressure he needed to get creative juices flowing.

Of course, your list doesn't have to be so ambitious. It may satisfy you to get this amount of work done in your life, but chances are if you can manage a fraction of Edison's "Idea Quota" you'll have things running smoothly and efficiently after a little while.

Take Notes

By writing your ideas and thoughts down on paper, you free your cognitive resources to stay focused on the task at hand. To date, five million pages of Edison's notes have been found and preserved. He used notes for many different purposes. He kept organized files so that he would never have to do the same research twice. He also kept to-do lists and reminders to keep him on task. He also had messy notes filled with mixed up inventions, attempts at poetry and calligraphy, and the occasional new idea. It seems as if he almost used paper as a medium for better expressing the workings of his brain and finding new ways to synthesize ideas.

Law 6

The 6th Law: Cut The Excess

"Waste is worse than loss. The time is coming when every person who lays claim to ability will keep the question of waste before him constantly. The scope of thrift is limitless."

- Thomas Edison

Prune away superfluous meetings (and their attendees).

Few activities are more of a productivity drain than meetings. If you must meet (and this should be a big "if"), make sure the agenda is prepared and everyone knows what needs to be accomplished before people are assembled. If people are present who don't help out with achieving that objective, let them leave. A relevant question to ask at the beginning of any meeting is "Do we all know why we're here?" and then follow that with, "Does everyone need to be here?" To trim the length of any meeting possible at any time, you can also try calling and assembling meetings in places not traditionally meant for meetings like a hall way or foyer. This will encourage people to get the pertinent information and move along. You can also get to the point and everyone out of the way quickly if you call a standing meeting.

Practice saying "No."

Creative energy is not infinite. Seasoned idea-makers know that they must guard their energy, and their focus closely. In no universe can a person expected to be all things to all people, and sometimes the correct answer is "no".

When is it the correct time to turn down an offer or decline a request? It's nice to be able to help someone and extend your generosity when you can, but if you stop what you're doing and help everyone and anyone you will constantly be distracted and prevented from completing your own tasks. Even worse, you are spending your resources, weather it is in the form of time or energy on a task that isn't your goal. You need to keep a healthy perspective of helping others and disengaging from things that don't directly benefit you. The time to say no is when an activity or charity is both keeping you from your task, and expending your energy in a way that is setting you back.

The most easily understood example for this concept is when a friend or family member asks you for money so that they can pay needed bill so they don't immediately lose their utilities. Your first impulse may be to say, yes, of course, I will always help my family when they ask. This is fine when you are able to meet their needs. However, if the next time they ask, you only have enough to pay your own utility bill, it is time to politely say no, so that what you may offer doesn't risk you losing your own utilities.

This also goes for your energy and time. If the energy or time being requested from you is taking your resources, so that you cannot meet your own responsibilities, then it is time to politely say no.

This can be tricky and uncomfortable, since you naturally want to help family, and you may feel pressure to always say yes to a boss. It is also tricky, because the party who is on the requesting end may not understand your limitations, and being rejected may provoke a variety of negative feelings. Saying no does not need be harsh or abrasive, but try to keep firm boundaries so that you can keep your responsibilities moving forward. When you're in execution mode, keep in mind that "unexpected opportunities" also mean distraction from the work at hand. Saying no is an essential part of the productivity equation.

Law 7

The 7th Law: Rule Maker, Not Rule Breaker

> "Hell, there are no rules here - we're trying to accomplish something."
>
> - Thomas Edison

Remember that rules, even productivity rules, are made to be broken.

Did we say develop a routine? This and other tips here should only be followed as long as they are *working*. If forward motion has become impossible with your current routine, try something else. Whether it's taking a long distance trip, popping into the gym in the middle of the day, walking around the block, or talking to a complete stranger at the morning coffee shop, make sure you occasionally shake up your normal routine. Breaking habits offers new perspective and helps recharge us to head back into the fray.

Make this thought personal? Is there an idea that could make you break that wall of hesitation and start acting on right now? Are there other rules of thumb you know of that you've found particularly useful for making ideas happen for you personally? Your ideas don't need to be traditional.

Thomas Edison endured all of twelve weeks of formal education in his life. Soon after he enrolled in school as a young child, his teacher complained that he was hyperactive and stupid. So Edison's mother pulled him out and taught him herself at home.

Edison viewed his lack of formal education as a blessing. He said it helped him to be innovative, to challenge assumptions. When tackling a new invention, Edison tested wildly. He often tried (and occasionally succeeded in creating) things that scientists considered impossible.

Don't be afraid of naps

Thomas Edison boasted that he slept for only a few hours each night and could work for three days straight. However, his dirty secret lied in an unusual ability to take power naps. Edison was famous for napping anywhere and everywhere. He sometimes napped for up to three hours, multiple times a day! One of his assistants insisted that his "genius for sleep equaled his genius for invention."

This ability to power nap allowed him the flexibility to get into the zone and work for incredibly long periods of time. He could charge up on sleep whenever it was convenient or whenever he needed a creative boost.

"The best thinking has been done in solitude.*" – Thomas Edison*

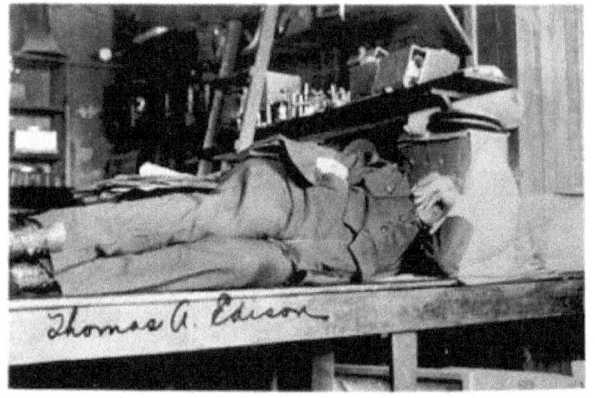

By the time you've realized that you are ready to break rules, or are in a position to be allowed to break rules, you must realize that critical thinking must be engaged thoroughly with this concept. Don't think of breaking rules in terms of power control or spiting a supervisor. Think in terms of whether or not tweaking the rules is going to provide you a benefit to meet your objective and make your accomplishment better. Is stopping work early and going to the gym keeping you from making technical mistakes because you have hit fatigue and you need to stop before you make an error in work? Or is leaving work early and hitting happy hour just a lazy move? The answers are up to you, but it is essential to use the "rule breaking" technique as a tool not an excuse.

Law 8

The 8th Law: Never Give Up & Do It Again

"Be courageous. I have seen many depressions in business. Always America has emerged from these stronger and more prosperous. Be brave as your fathers before you. Have faith! Go forward!"
--Thomas Edison

Since Thomas Edison was home schooled, primarily because of the way his mother was displeased with how he was treated at school when his teachers were quoted as saying "he's too stupid to learn anything," his sense of identity was molded at an early age. Due to his partial deafness he was labeled as dumb by school administration. Later in Edison's life he was fired by his first two employers for the accusation of being non-productive. Thankfully, the support of his mother didn't let this misfortune affect his self-esteem. She constantly promoted his more valuable qualities that encouraged him to seek his success without falling victim to the harsh words of the outside world. Edison was left with the sentiment,

"Our greatest weakness lies in giving up. The most certain way to succeed is to try one more time." – Thomas Edison

One of Edison's biggest failures was the invention of cement furniture. At the Edison Portland Cement Company in 1899, they made everything from cabinets, couches, and even houses from cement construction. The idea was a disaster. The furniture was uncomfortable. It usually crumbled as soon as it was delivered, and concrete was too expensive at its time to justify making the entire contents of a house from that material. The idea was a complete flop, and soon went out of business, of course, not before the company was hired to build Yankee Stadium in the Bronx.

Thomas Edison was the epitome of perseverance. He even claimed to have tried thousands of different filaments before finding a cheap, but reliable substance to use for his electric light bulbs.

Forget talent, genius is hard work

"Genius is hard work, stick-to-itiveness, and common sense." – Thomas Edison

Edison claimed that he was not born particularly talented. He was a firm believer in hard work and perseverance. It was character traits and good habits that made him successful, not some sort of genius gene.

What if you just aren't as creative as him? Edison also claimed that "invention is two percent inspiration and 98 percent perspiration." Those who knew him insisted he had zero tolerance for lazy people.

"Never write yourself off because you aren't as smart or creative as the great successes around you. All you need to be great is hard work."

"There is no substitute for hard work."

"Many of life's failures are people who did not realize how close they were to success when they gave up."

– Thomas Edison

Conclusion

Over the years Edison has been harshly criticized on some of his personal choices. He accomplished an almost unbelievable number of projects in his lifetime. If there is such a thing as being too productive, Edison would be the perfect example. He was so focused on work that his family suffered for it. He was not close to any of his children. In fact, one of his son's used aliases all his life because he felt so disconnected from his father that he did not want to be associated with him.

Not only did Edison's family often suffer a loss with his absence, but his employees were overworked, and not always given the credit due to them. Edison was so focused on success and invention, that he became overly competitive and sometimes resorted to shady deals and idea theft to get ahead.

While Edison isn't a perfect role model (nobody is perfect), no one can deny that he knew a thing or two about getting things done. By taking his mantras and life lessons without his all overly extreme gusto, perhaps we can learn something and push ourselves forward to better productivity.

Edison was a power house of creativity and invention, and undeniably incredibly productive. Edison received 1093 patents in his lifetime, an all-time record. What is even more amazing? Almost every single one of his patents are tied to commercial successes. Want a sampling of some of the industries Edison influenced? Well, he invented the phonograph and kick-started the recorded music industry which is now worth over 150 billion dollars. He created the company General Electric after inventing a marketable electric light. He experimented with batteries and portable energy. He also invented moving pictures and kick-started iron ore mining, telecommunications, office and copying technology, cement, and electrochemical therapy.

How in the world did Edison fit so much creativity and invention into one lifetime? Here are more of the personal success principles that he followed:

Stay in touch with your customers

We all know Thomas Edison as America's great inventor, but some don't know that he was also a marketing guru. In 1869, Edison invented an electronic vote counter with the ability to greatly reduce the hassle and time it took to vote. To his astonishment, the counter turned out to be a huge flop. Why? Because legislatures didn't want efficient voting. They wanted time for deliberation and lobbying. From that early failure, Edison realized that his inventions must fix his customer's real problems, not the problems that he assumed they would have.

"Anything that won't sell, I don't want to invent. Its sale is proof of utility, and utility is success ". – Thomas Edison

He forced himself to refrain for inventing anything purely for the sake of inventing it. Instead, he went out and found real problems people were frustrated with and designed his inventions to solve those problems.

Don't work alone

One of Edison's greatest inventions was the method he used to invent. He designed a dream laboratory and filled it with talented men, giving them the freedom to explore their own ideas. He built his space with huge open rooms where people could talk and work. There were no set hours, but all the men worked long and hard and seemed to enjoy it. It was, in a sense, the first research and development lab. Apple and Google both model their headquarters after Edison's famous wizards park.

A lot of people compare Thomas Edison and Nikola Tesla. While Tesla was most certainly a brilliant inventor, he did not come near Edison in invention output over his life time. One of the key differences between them was that Tesla insisted on working alone, whereas Edison had the advantage of a team of guys helping him to get more done in less time.

Do what you enjoy

"I never did a day's work in my life. It was all fun." – Thomas Edison

Edison set high expectations for himself. His friends and family accused him of being a workaholic, and for good reason. However, he didn't see it that way. He genuinely loved inventing. In fact, he claimed that he really didn't work at all. He enjoyed everything that he did. So if you want to be successful, find something you are passionate about and pursue it with every ounce of strength in your being.

Other Books in the 8 Laws Series

Book 1: The Leadership: 8 Laws of Leadership: Develop Your Team, Influence & Inspire Others, & Lead People with Success

Book 2: The Saving: 8 Laws of Saving Money: Budgeting Your Savings and Debt, Managing Your Personal Finance That Doesn't Suck

Book 3: Happiness: The 8 Laws of Happiness: Steps to a Happy Lifestyle & Family on a Joyful Journey with the Fueled Success of Positive Thinking

Book 4: Time management: The 8 Laws of Time Management: Increase Your Productivity with Time Management Skills & Get Things Done in Less Time with These Techniques

Book 5: Courage: Develop Confidence and Overcome Fear Like a Boss

Book 6: Kindness: The 8 Laws of Kindness: The Powerful Benefit That Leads Us To Success Through Loving Compassion

Book 7: Power: The 8 Laws of Power

Book 8: Productivity: The 8 Laws of Productivity: Learn to be More Productive and get More Done to Increase Success

Book 9: Learning: The 8 Laws of Learning

Book 10: Communication: The 8 Laws of Communication

www.ingramcontent.com/pod-product-compliance
Lightning Source LLC
Chambersburg PA
CBHW060410190526
45169CB00002B/839